Polishing The Evidence

CECILIA MCGOVERN

salmonpoetry

Published in 2008 by
Salmon Poetry,
Cliffs of Moher, County Clare, Ireland
Website: www.salmonpoetry.com
Email: info@salmonpoetry.com

ISBN 978-1-903392-99-7

Cover artwork: Jane McGovern
Cover design & Typesetting: Siobhán Hutson

the arts
council
an chomhairle
ealaíon

For My Family

Acknowledgments & Thanks

Acknowledgements are due to the editors of the following publications where some of the poems included here, or versions of them, have been previously published:

The Sunday Tribune, *Poetry Ireland Review* and *Womens'Work Anthology IV*.

"Dispersal" and "Harvest" won prizes in the Dun Laoghaire Poetry Festival; "Wedding Photo" in the National Women's Poetry Competition

The author would like to thank the following for their help and encouragement:

Finola Flanagan, Professor Andrew Carpenter, Thornfield Poets, Renate Ahrens-Kramer, Sheila Barrett, Alison Dye, Catherine Phil MacCarthy, Joan O'Neill and Julie Parsons.

Contents

Polishing The Evidence

*"It would take a whole book to chart the brilliant deviations
the voice can take to prevent its owner from being known"*

IRIS WARREN, Voice Teacher

Beside Lough Lannagh

Petal and leaf dust on familiar paths,
damp heat from hedgerows,
we try to name shrubs and trees,
sure only of the rowan
with its pinnate leaves.

Is it elder or hazel,
honeysuckle or woodbine?
An emigrant most of life,
you call a tall buttercup
The Greater Celandine.

Unused names come to mind
from schoolbook and song
coll, feithle, trom, fuinnseog;
on palate, deep in throat,
the long vowels echo.

The Coothrements

What was broken
and wouldn't mend
gleamed, half embedded
in the "Coothrements" [*],
a grassy mound at a gable end.

My childish hand longed to risk
nettles sting and crawling slime,
sift through flinty shards,
recreate the pattern in china
or haggled-over ornaments.

But from somewhere
reverberations of damage,
the splintering crash,
the "marbh fhaisc ort"
a stifled language hurled

in reproach for a precious thing,
awkwardly lost.

[*] "Coothrements": In Mayo, a dump for
broken china, ornaments and glass.

Polishing The Evidence

Irish poetry and song
at the Festival Hall,
coloured lights on the boardwalk,
April dusk over the white span
of Waterloo.

You point out the buildings,
St. Bride's, St. Paul's,
"dwarfed by the new ugliness,
streetscapes stolen", you say,
pained, proprietary.

Gone the breathy consonants
of a Mayo childhood,
your accent clear and clipped
as the veiled lady's
who ruled a church pew,

whose demesne wall we climbed
Sunday afternoons
scuffing our good shoes,
dogs going wild. Back home
we polished away the evidence.

June Drownings

A hot day in early June
their feet reluctant to leave
the no-man's-land
of dusty headland grass,
lush beside the pale earth
of endless drills they must weed
to do their father's will

Their eyes stray
from wilting turnip tops,
follow shimmering air
across to the Reek.
Beyond it, acres of ocean
but nearer Lough Lannagh's waters
stretch all the way to town.

Soil-dried hands drop clothes
for their father to find,
past the drills
he furrowed straight,
past the narrow path to the lake,
all weed-choked now in July
at the Month's Mind.

A child, envious of the attention
death conferred, I follow
unnoticed, adults who need
to know as distance and depth
the exact spot at "The Point"
where the boy cousins I never met
entered the lake.

Stones At A Roundabout

(i.m. Sr Agnes)

The out-of-town developer bought
the convent you entered after Leaving Cert.,
a listed building, burnt by night
marauders while developer
and town looked the other way.

He also bought
the chapel where you took your vows,
prostrate on the sanctuary steps, risked
the coldness of stone,
the deadness of copied stained glass;

the chapel stones, soon to be
a boundary wall,
rest briefly, a memorial cairn
or marker on a funeral path
near the latest roundabout.

He also bought the graves,
yours and a century and a half's
dead sisters. The church said prayers
while the bones that shaped
unglimpsed flesh were exposed.

At The Museum Of Country Life

My childhood is here among familiar farm tools.
Untarnished by earth, the work of subsistence or survival,
cartwheels wont wobble, hayrakes become gap-toothed.
As much a throwback as a Bronze Age metal-worker,
beside a glasscase of torcs and amulets, I watch children
queue for touchscreen quizzes on farm life, lose interest in
seconds.

Ask myself can pristine tools and perfectly woven baskets
for one hundred euros link now to then, the people, the
life, tell us anything of their struggle. They would laugh
at the idea of unused tools sitting in a room.

Money floodlights the round tower, builds the white
modern building. But what of the gap-toothed hayrake of
history, the silence that lasted more than a hundred years.
What of the time, a "society wedding", my father saying
"you are the first person in this family to set foot in that
house", the gatekeepers wife and myself, both adrift, strike
up a conversation.

And others *had* set foot there, entered the library,
walked to the steward's table, rent money and cap in hand.

Known World

After a mean century
they trundled
a swaying cartload
down from the foothills

their survival unspoken
except what you glean
from a stone dwelling
roofless, ivied over,

steps to a grain loft,
a door you must stoop
to enter, but young,
cannot, uneasy with

the place, the history
the known deaths –
childbirth, not hunger –
a famine of tenderness.

ii

Great grandfather
Great Famine survivor
signed with an "X"
lived beyond ninety.

A Fir Bolg man
carried bags of soil,
built the grain loft,
six steps from damp and rats.

Like a vessel facing disaster,
ditched the non-essential,
his language,
naturalness;

spoke the words
of a school primer,
of his children's future,
held his mother tongue.

iii

Grandfather,
photographed in sunlight,
moustached, dark clothes,
leaning on a whitewashed wall.

Greek looking,
my sister said, needing
to uplift us with
exotic possibilities.

School, a new language
weaned the old, fully,
off the tip of his tongue,
his children spoke none;

fitted him
for migrant worker,
able to calculate
crop seed and acreage.

Sixty, twice wifeless,
not yet head of the house;
the famine survivor,
his tongue loosed

still there
signing "X"
in the second census
of the twentieth century.

iv

Father,
mornings, late summer, first up,
a distant closeness;
your weather-eyes on
the haze over Nephin's foothills
the first home you hardly spoke of;
brushing against

overnight webs
linking branches
in the orchard you helped plant,
we search for the pastel-blush
of late Beauties of Bath,
eat them sliced on bread.

Now I would say
take my hand and go
where your eyes linger,
mountain ash held to the slope
by fibrous roots,
Nephin's bulk above us;

my hand will tighten
for the woman dying
in childbirth,
an absence never spoken,
heard in your dying words
"Dad, dad, lift me up".

Conversation Rules

"So you're off to General Franco's country"
spoken by the man who lived behind newspapers;

all we never said, years of words
hostage to unspoken rules

ignored by my sister when she inquired
the nature of the case one time you were a juror.

The snap of tensely-held paper,
taut as your voice "the same as many another".

Now I think what if ......the table cleared,
seated sideways at the head

you folded the paper; as lovingly as you could
tried to recount the unloving courtroom story,

how the clatter of delph, rasp of tongs would cease
our caught-up breath release, a door inch open.

Element of Uncertainty

Framed in teakwood
clear as air,
all that stood
between the sparrowhawk,
and the afterlife
of a stuffed bird

the window she smashed
herself against, full tilt
from the conifers,
to swoop on the white cat
somnolent
on the sofa back.

Like glass, the wall
that drops between us
when talk edges close;
I search for the door
here...there...not there,
remember the sparrowhawk.

The Missing "O"

That O now, a Boston ganger said
during the Depression
to my uncle by marriage James O'Connor,
there's something you could do without.

On the other hand, you could
if you had a mind to,
stick an "s" on the end
to make up for it.

This is why my yank first cousins
the Connors
have first cousins in Mayo,
the O'Connors.

Twelve

That summer held me
at arm's length,
overgrown,
meant to be of use,
standing useless
in a doorway

watching holidays ebb
along the grey houses
of a one-sided street
into the mid-distance,
the bright patchy tar
of the road home.

Seeing, now and then,
a child, coins in fist,
race to the shop
to stain lurid colours
of bruises and blood
on lips and teeth;

once, all halldoors closed,
a bell single-tolling,
a hearse, low-sprung,
snake from the church,
girls my age
among the first mourners.

I saw the future then,
my childhood summers over;
mother taking the air
in Enniscrone, older in sealight.
"You're pale" she said,
as if seeing me a first time.

Soul Thoughts

I have never dreamt of my soul
not in the slant-life dramas
that wake with me and vanish
between one thought and the next.

Mine was last
in the family soul lottery,
a younger brother, born
soulless, without breath,

barred from consecrated ground,
buried in a field corner
forever fallow.
Is soul breath?

When I shared mother's bed
snug against her long back
she prayed "to breathe forth
her soul in peace".

I fell asleep, listening
to the small rhythmic "puh"
of her lips on out-breath,
too weak to wing the lightest soul.

A Season For Everything

Earth sliced, sticky clábar
crows skydive for worms,
my father throws
the odd backward glance.
My eye is on primroses
threatened by the headland turn
of plough and horse.

He walks easily
after the swaying harrow,
the plough noses up drills,
lime and manure sting
hands and nostrils.
I lug buckets of slits
calculate distances.

Light Autumn earth,
root tendrils snap
under the fork,
potatoes gleam white
in the dusk. I am cold.
I wear his jacket,
hands high in the sleeves.

Dark earth heaped on grass,
their colours mock
the undertaker's green cover
as if it could shield him,
meeting earth now
without spade or plough.

Drinking Water

i

Allowed alone
down the well's stone steps,
too intent on my task
to stare Narcissus-like,

lower the shiny can sideways.
My image fractures and undulates.
I weave the can to avoid
floating embryos of caonach.

ii

Most deadly
when it coursed fever
and fear through my home town.
Typhoid. Child deaths.

Forgotten a decade later
when I press my lips
to the outlet of a pump,
crank the iron arm

as the townies did.
Surprised at not a trickle.
Withdraw my mouth. Suddenly
a live eel slaps the concrete path.

I stare at the taut-muscled body,
like me, out of his element,
listen for the jeers, me
and the eel in almost intimacy.

iii

Ten years ago, maybe still,
a country lane in summer;
in the hedge above a roadside well,
a cup for the thirsty traveller
who would dare drink.

Kneading Belief

Captive to half-made bread
you stand against the table
sticky hands in a rhythm

reach, sprinkle, stir; pause
while a half-fistful of flour
strips interlaced fingers.

All the time, your lips silently
retell some bitterness or pray
some troubled entreaty.

I kneel on a chair
thinking up an interruption.
"Do you believe in the Blessed Trinity?"

Never slackening rhythm,
a nod and emphatic "I do"
kneads belief into bread

you dust into a circle,
carve with a deep cross
before placing in the oven.

Brittleness

That freezing winter, we discovered
the brittleness of icicles,
a row of hilted daggers saved
from sunlight
behind a hayshed, bordered
closely by a hedge

We lifted them off galvanised iron
brandished them like fighting
Gallowglasses in our history book;
the point shattered at first touch,
the hilt almost welded
to our fingers, we ran,

stretched red-blue hands
to be rubbed better.
Your hands in a basin of dough
we stretched them to the fire,
cried with the pain of frozen
fingers ungently warmed.

Dark Interiors

The potter turns a wide bowl,
a half-formed hemisphere,
his forearms caked with clábar;

familiar sludge I leaped over
in winter gaps, cycled
fast through in potholes,
legs aloft from splashes.

The bowl set to dry,
hands washed, he sells me
some glazed and patterned
Mayo clay
to take back to the city

a sugar bowl, jug,
and six mugs whose dark
interiors will do nothing for
the amber translucence of tea,
the opaque depths of coffee;

that clutter one end of a sideboard
while I take out china cups.

Close as I'll ever be to saying
Go raibh maith agat a Mhaigh Eo.

Beyond Telling

Even black and white film caught something of your flame-coloured hair, its strong texture framing the paleness of your face, your waif-like stance. Up steps with classmates, the steps you fell down injuring your back, a hurt never told out of pity, too strong, too soon, shows up years later as chipped bone.

Your name on no benefit list in this country, you fly Luton-Knock in summer. We joke about meeting on the gable. Talk again of that first outward journey, a parcel of bacon for a neighbour hidden in your headscarf at Customs.

Hearing the self-mockery, the loneliness, I think of the moment when your spine hit stone, of other moments of raw memory: mother absent; your tense oldest-child face. A life of exile, the randomness of what's given.

Underwater Explorer

Missing
from the shower room
in the turn of a head,
when I found my three year old
under the surface
of the swimming pool
not out of her element
no struggle or panic,
the slipstream of her hair
combed by water
was pure terror.

Levelling

The westwind swept
unchecked through
the thinned-out evergreens,
flattened the last apple tree.

It lies eastwards,
crown to earth, as if
listening for an aftershock,
an echo of the almost uprooting.

The seasons still visit,
cover it now in white blossom,
the radiance of holy people
near death, of you

bondswoman to earth,
shoulders and back work-slanted
falling here, on a last errand,
face in orchard grass.

Tempting Providence

When, in childhood, I said
on some inert day
whose particles struggled
with weak purpose towards night,
"I wish something would happen",
Mother would say
"May God forgive you!

Dark Stirrings

A fall of tentacles,
ivory, veined with mauve,
clogs the sink.

Brush in hand, I survey
the damage, end of a bag's
dark stirrings.

Feel the heaviness,
nurture and betrayal
bred in the bone,

my father, battle-tense,
seated among baskets
and sacks, judges

which eyes will sprout,
carves potatoes into slits,
knife cuts towards the palm.

Easter, a blight on running free,
hardly a glimpse of sky,
eyes on a grid of furrows.

Half impelled, I dig
and plant heavy suburban soil
without leaven of manure or lime.

Cheered by tall green stalks,
harvest them early. Hear a voice,
" Waste. Too soon. Only poirins"

The Flaw

Its branches, weighed down
under another season's crop,
remind me of my resolve
to prune this tree,
give it a winter wash.

Too late,
it has overfruited,
multiplying damage
under a skin
wine red, enticing.

It discomfits me
to sit near, to know
that the first bite
could uncover the flaw,
the telltale slug hole.

If you don't believe
what you can scarcely see,
you will find yourself
looking down a black tunnel,
the beginning already
in your mouth.

Waning

The moon's wispy hairpiece
disappears down the sky
behind the hospital,
leaves a half-dissolved face
in a dome of blue.

In your upstairs ward,
a pale blue cap on her head,
her body the weight
of a nine year old's,
a woman sits by the window

leaning intently forward,
hands and eyes folded
she tracks what consumes
the toing and froing
the trees, the sky

and the waning moon
who can remake
from sliver of jaw
a full face.

Crematorium

'Crematorium' and 'Columbarium' –
words that sound like Latin sentences.

The curtained opening in the chapel wall
behind which your coffin rests, could be
the kitchen hatch where you stood,
hands poised to offer your best delph teapot
to complete the supper tray.

Or the half-curtained windows
of the pub alcove where you,
the punctual one, waited;
where we formed a confiding circle,
swopping our life stories.

I sense the threatening heat
behind the chapel's coldness,
remembering how we almost perished
by heat in Sr. Rosario's class,
hot afternoons.

All windows closed,
knuckles gnarled and knotted,
immobile fingers clamping
the textbook, Sr. Rosario sat
wrapped in rugs in her wheelchair.

"Amo, amas, amat", we droned
while Summer hummed outside. Her
pain controlled our restlessness. We
eased burning cheeks on the cool tin
of our pencil cases. The priest hastily

intones the final prayers. My body
jerks, involuntarily I nudge
an empty space, as your coffin glides.
Your orderly mind would
have approved this smooth exit.

Outside, the empty hearse is still
festooned with flowers. Mourners
chat in groups like after Sunday mass
and the April sun reveals empty spaces
on the columbarium wall.

*'Crematorium' and 'Columbarium' –
words that sound like Latin sentences.*

Ticking Over

Our centrifugal force stepped
into the train, never looked back.
Things realigned.
The dresser tightened
against the wall.
The table was longer.
We circled each other.

Next day's light duly brightened,
I watched you do
her morning work,
louder metal-clanking
thicker clouds of ash motes,
bread sliced as if sawing wood.

Teatime, I read aloud,
risked interrupting
the line by line perusal
of the local paper.
Without lifting your eyes
you corrected my pronunciation
not lo-*com*-otive, lo-co-*mot*-ive.

Salvage

By-child,
the old people's word,
offspring of a kitchen maid
and a son of the manor.

Not fully ignored.
After politics torched the house,
a gift of silver platters
salvaged from the fire.

Tarnished, unbreakable,
hens fed from them
outside a dwelling
without bed, chair, table.

Homeward Bound

Built-up order behind me, here and there fence posts
askew; to my left, a swan in full-breasted ease on the canal
bank; past white crosses for journeys cut short, towns by-
passed for speed, their streets a memory and soon, up
ahead, an immensity of sky that made a child I loved cry
for the city's protection.

The stop, the fake English shopfronts lining the walkway
to the rear of the hotel. Over the Shannon at Tarmonbarry,
the legendary coming-down in the world, king to beggar,
hell or Connaught; the bridge lifts for a queue of boats
going down or upriver, the pilot turns the lever that can
raise tons of concrete, drop them back without a space.

My rearview mirror shows the tense face of the next
stalled driver. He drums the knuckles of his right hand on
his car roof. This is how we accommodate, when there's
no way forward, sometimes have to construct a makeshift,
test it against our weight. Fearful of scuttling everything,
gather up the pieces you can bear, fit them into as coherent
a picture as you can, to a pattern of scarcely, about workable,
forge ahead, blinkered to the periphery.

What happened where I'm going besides birth, the
ache that wants a re-run, a second chance, flat plains
behind, first sight of the mountains, beyond them the
ocean, endless, cold, needing summer light.

A Different Cold

Children who had never seen snow
saved some in the freezer
the winter of '82.
Dazzling snowlight unified
the landscape, brought
the mountains nearer.

You were seventeen,
your gangly frame lost
in the padded serge
of an army overcoat;
a trail of bootprints
to your girlfriend's house
broken for an old man

about to lose his footing
on a glassy slope.
With one hand
being tall
and seemingly strong,
you gripped his lapels,
steadied him against a wall.

It's said a quarter of the old
dont survive a fall,
...but this talk
of a man neither of us knew
or the brief brilliance
of that winter cannot
stave off what follows

the thaw
the ordinary weather
that leads
where I don't want to go –
to October,
to a different cold.

Ebb and Flow

Late lamb,
child of my middle years,
we look for likenesses
in photographs.

Here I am your age
eleven, flat chested
a shy field and wood sprite
suntanned at summer's end

only some garbled words away
from the red leakage,
Parturition's minions
at work, setting up house;

the dismantlings
as she departed,
echoes of her coming,
shook the whole structure.

From this ebb-tide shore,
I watch you, my daughter
enter the lunar sway.
Your eyes look past me.

My Daughter's Hands

A bowlful of familiar hands,
not in a court of summary justice

here, wax-cast, organ-pink
on the kitchen windowsill

delicate piano fingers
the smallest crooked highest

unlined palm upwards,
fingers spread in appeal

linear, thumb angled wide
to interlock friendship

fisted, a toddler's find
needing to be gently prised.

Always the chill of open wrists
until she's there

beside her cloned hands
marvellously unposthumous

hair newly magenta
slim fingers rolling a cigarette.

Dispersal

A membership card
with your signature falls
from the bag you borrowed,
unfolds on the words Organ Donor.
I retrieve it as though
it were a leprous thing

knowing I could never
want you less than whole
my just-grown daughter,
never share your fearsome
generosity with the body
this body nurtured;

reminded of predators who invade
the bone-temple of their prey
in search of the vitals;
the heap of coiled entrails
one early morning in the front garden
with not a scrap of feather or fur;

a sheep's heart with its lopped
arteries and veins in the school lab.,
the human heart mislaid
on a hospital shelf. Everything
that lives, at the mercy
of the forces of dispersal.

I turn to a photograph to find
the untransplantable,
the essence of you, warm
myself in the steady flame
of your eyes.

Avian War

I wake to rattling roof tiles
above my attic bedroom,
feet hurrying
purposefully.

Battle resumes,
loot is fought over,
dropped hostages
thud downwards.

Hurried pursuit.
Raucous cries.
Silence.
Sinister tapping;

a shell breached
by a gristly beak,
the glup as a soft body
is gorged.

Half-asleep, I dream
bird ambushes,
a bright sprinkle
of crumbs on snow

under a low-sided basket
propped on a stick,
string from the stick
to my brother's hand.

To A Swan On A Boatslip

Is it worth it
for some scattered bread
to lose the majesty
of water and you conjoined

swing your rear end
up the boatslip
like a portly arthritic;
lower and twist

the proud prow
of your neck to forage
among hysterical gulls
on permanent take-off.

Three cygnets, still colour-
barred aim threatening pecks
everywhere as if they sense
a fall from grace.

Glandular Fever

Dry heat surged through your body,
climaxed in drenched clothes,
sapped teenage anger,
you were soft spoken, tractable.

No miracle drug,
a scene from an old film,
pillows on a chair, I kept vigil,
cooled your face, supported your steps,

haunted by lines
from a remembered poem
"the hectic brighter daily
and the death dew on her hair".

Suddenly desiring
a dreaded future,
you on the bedside chair,
our linked walking.

Looking After

The spirit, at times of threat to the body, absconds,
looks back from a height, as if to say
clay was never its element

She would not remember
that ordinary day fading
into evening, in school dress,
head bowed over homework,
vaguely aware of the man
working in the bedroom.

It begins the moment
when her aunt securing her hat
with a pin, the blunt end a pearl,
ready for Devotions,
announces with airy lightness
her enigmatic piece
about niece and repairman
looking after each other.

Called to the bedroom
to hand him something,
she sees herself pushed
backwards onto the bed,
neck muscles at war
with gravity, face turning
from a mouth
of perfect false teeth.

Angels' Plot

Can these other-worldly little ones
crowded under headstones,
hear the lullaby in wind chimes
the song of metal mobiles
the poem in plastic sleeve
nailed to a tree;

see the names inscribed
on dancing stockings and santas,
soft animals, free of milk smells
dipping down saplings;
imagine the faithful hearts
who remember them this dream?

"A Mayo Peasant Boy"

(Portrait by Patrick Tuohy)

Limpid eyes look straight
half expecting blame,
a grimy purple homespun,
broad wrists and hands
tell of a working childhood.

He could be sitting
in a school desk, ready
to submit to wood or leather,
no maistin[*], barely a quiver
of his indented lower lip.

My brother
you might have looked like this,
set me on a different path,
no longer the lowly youngest,
taught me the ways of infants.

The church which allotted you
a stillborn's grave,
lately discovered its human heart,
baptised a handful of clay,
gave you a name nobody speaks.

Hedges, ditches and corners
have yielded to the tractor.
Taking a diagonal from the gate
through the crater of a sand pit,
helps me locate you.

[*] Maistin: In Mayo, a cry-baby.

Dock Labour Board

...three words that stood out
in a conversation
that excluded her twice,
as female and as child.

She puzzled over them.
Dock was a tall weed
that turned a crumbly brown.
Labour was master

over cold, over the hurt
of hessian-burnt knees
latticed red from weeding
along furrows shorter

in halves. Or so he said,
a trick on labour perfected
in a working childhood
before he left roadside docks

to hoist goods on Mersyside;
the unprodigal eldest, waiting
to claim his inheritance,
bring it his labour's love.

Spent, at day's end, the local
weekly, taut as a board, fenced
off the space across his chest
where a child could nestle.

Wedding Photo

There is a sense of destiny fulfilled.
Framed by potted plants, she sits
clasping her marriage scroll, he
apologetically stands.
A photo contrived
as their romance, balanced
in the matchmaker's scales, his
reputation for hard work, her
sewing and cooking skills.
I search the picture
for clues to lost loves
far-off childhoods and find
a man in a well-cut suit
a woman in a stylish outfit and
two pairs of mud-splashed shoes

Lisaniska

(Depopulated in a mass eviction sometime between 1841-1851)

I look for them in the state archives, across cobbled
Henrietta Street, past the grime-blackened houses of their
rich contemporaries, under the arch to Land Registry,
searching for proof of the story of a poker game between
landlords – my village gambled, lost. In a heat-controlled
room, lift down weighty record books, pink covers frayed,
search the stylish script in vain for a title deed with
Lisaniska's name.

At Ancient Maps, surrender portable possessions – a
pen could be a camera – unfold table-sized parchment,
find it 1839, name unchanged.

Microfilm in the National Library flashes the barely
legible print of the Connaught Ranger: The Queen at
Balmoral. Upcoming levees. Births, "to the lady of John
Black, a son and heir".

Page long advertisements for Syriacum, the cordial
balm that cured Mr Wytham Baxter of "constipation of
the bowels which application to literary pursuits had long
entailed upon him".

Poetry – a literate subject enraptured at the birth of a
royal heir – "Proclaim, proclaim, a prince hath burst the
womb". Love poems replete with "whence... thou dost...
o'er the main".

No mention of thirty four houses levelled, two hundred
and four people who fell out of history, a Christmas Eve
in the darkest decade; in their place, a herdsman's cottage,
six people, cattle for England.

After it all, nothing to add to delph fragments, to the
stone of ruined houses in field walls; to family names van-
ished from the parish register; to a sense of presence, my
hand about to pick wild strawberries.

Harvest

The youngest held the stick,
tidying and slanting the grainheads
for the scythe swing,
learning the art
of not getting in the way.
Child's work.

The lifter laid neat bundles
complete with bands
readymade for the binder
to twist and secure
into finished sheaves.

A necessary pause
while the elongated oval
of the whetstone rasped
the cutting edge;

juicy Victorias straight
from the orchard
slaked our thirst,
their smooth skins balm
to corn-chapped hands.

Walking home at dusk
the stooked sheaves
we had masterminded
huddled symmetrically
and stubble nicked
the exposed skin
of our feet.

First Communicant

Soul must be shining
venial sins rehearsed;
disobedience, lies

and a holy picture
found under a desk, kept
for the angel with yellow hair

not for the strange words
"lest thou dash thy foot".
It was never a foot

always knees
on stone chippings
mortal-sin size cuts

like lips that ate glass.
Teacher alarmed
"child, that needs a stitch"

pressing them closed
between thumb and forefinger,
sent home with big sister.

Mortal knees
pockmarked white
for all mortality.

Connecting

(i.m. Dorothy Molloy)

We bounce words between us, finger car keys,
connect on "childhood", a palimpsest of place
fainter for you because abandoned sooner,
the forties West,

still there in the seaweed baths at Enniscrone,
iron smudges on enamel, a shower
with clanking pullchain. First,
sensitise the pores in a coffin

of a steambox. Trust in the hand controls
only the face visible. Waiting
heaped on the bath floor, seaweed
abundant enough to harbour shore life,

releases its good oil under heat,
brings to mind your writing credo
"Go deeper. Deeper.
The answer is always to go deeper"

Holiday Reunion

Rainy light through
a deep-set window.
Beyond it, what's left
of a once loved orchard,
a last half-uprooted tree
that leans its stunted crop.

Morning sounds,
monotone radio,
clank of cutlery,
the practical ones at work.
It is up to everyone
to make this a success,

find a way
on home ground, past
the sure sense of direction,
the back turned to swallow pills
to the children we were.
Let absent voices drift in

and a tongs rasp
through ashy embers
while I count ceiling boards
with a rote learner's obsession,
stains and knots for markers,
one blink and I'm lost.

The next generation
is adrift from all of this,
it will mostly die with us.

Gifts

At the time of your birth
the swallows huddled
plumage slack
on telephone wires;

the dart and swoop
the thin cries
of their skyfest ended,
hoarding strong wings

for the long haul,
low over land, alert
for sustenance
before the blank face of the desert.

Their instinct to go mysterious
as the instinct to be born
that began your journey at leaf-fall,
overdue, ripe as late fruit;

outside the window
feathered voyagers
with gifts of listening intently,
strength to face blankness.

Orange Blossom Birthday

Your twenty-first come,
over on the Pacific coast,
search and you might find
not just any shrub
of the genus *Citrus*,
a real orange tree.

Walking past clapboard houses
feeling the pride and heft of majority,
air sweet with familiar scent,
quickly snap a twig and run
as you did in childhood, clutching
a fistful of something seasonal.

At a safe distance, examine it,
not for bugs our shrub was host to,
the sinewy Dermaptera
you feared would worm
a passage to your brain
but for tiny orbs of light.

Trappings

They wait for you
this lavishly stocked house
and its colony
of sculpted animals and birds,
unaware you have
entered a parallel stillness
to raffia swans, stone herons,
ceramic cats in varied poses.

My hand recoils
from feathered things
that obstruct window catches,
lurk among photographs;
a story of immigrants,
back to the first stocky groom
and his docile bride.

Would they think
this luxury house,
the great-granddaughter
who vowed to cast off
religion and all its trappings,
a vindication of exile?

At the sky-blue hot tub
two live cats whose portraits
hang in my bedroom, doze
beside stone snails,
heads extruded eternally
while a sporadic breeze thrums
the wind-chime's wooden tongue.

Sunshower

It lands softly
a drop here, a drop there,

it darkens stones
before I feel anything;

on leaves, it's the sound
of popping fuchsia pods

the rustle of a presence
that sets me free to wonder.

It stops just as mysteriously.

The birds set about
their songs again

the pigeon's throaty depth
clearer in the freshened air

against the drip...drip
off trees and roofs.

The Darkest Hour

The echo of a sound in my ears
I assess each creak in the lurking dark,

envy the sleep of childhood
how the atoms of a small body settle

evenly, while mine permeable to my own
and others' woes, collide

in guts, in leg muscles tensed
to run me out where no-one is yet risen.

Out into a lane with walls high as roofs
where once, during the darkest hour

a man went from one yard door
to the next, thumping wood, crying.

I lay there wondering
what it would take of courage

or foolishness to open the door
on the abyss of that sorrow.

Voiceless

You twist a pencil in the grooves
of the soundless tape
the yoga teacher made
to get you through the summer,
the revolutions too feeble
to support a voice.

Reminded of the tumour operation;
the doctor, proud of its success,
invites you to watch your mother,
bald still along the scarline,
identify common objects,
gloves, a book, a hat.

You're back at the kitchen table,
finger-stepping words,
her lips shaping the first letter,
as yours do now.
Spotted by the surgeon-teacher:
"Really, if you must prompt....
please wait outside".

Erosion

What the cliff concedes
or the sea appropriates
deep in the frothing rush
of each successive wave

can only be gauged
on calm days,
an unwilled pact,
time and a face

that ages
in a photo album
leafed through idly
generations on.

The Mammogram

There's a cold blue on walls and carpet
even the trim on the radiographers jacket
and her eyes veer sideways
as mine did, when mother asked me
to paint iodine on her asthmatic chest.

Half-naked, as mother was, I raise
my chin to the chin rest,
the hopeful way animals look over fences,
shoulders hunched around steel,
steel myself for the clamp.

While the radiographer scurries
to the switch, if I faint to the floor
will the clamped member detach
as a preventative measure?

I want the changing blues of the sky,
green symphony of plants and trees,
flower urns overflowing
shocking-pink, cerise, vermilion.

Madwoman

Her brother was a married man.
She was a bush in the gap,
redundant, becoming strange.
He had no choice
what else could he do?
When the nurses came in
she said "Billy is the patient".

I was eight or nine. All I knew
of her then or since
that she gave rise to a joke
spread by her brother to his wife
the wife to a neighbour
the neighbour to a shopkeeper
the shopkeeper to a customer.

I remember the fear
when my mother laughed.

Eye Dream

My right eye felt looser
than expected so I took it out
for safe keeping. (Awake too,
I try to anticipate disaster.)

As the eye is astigmatic,
the problem was less visionary
than aesthetic. Sunglasses helped
hide the vacancy.

Knowing how I'd recoil
from the slithery feel of it
as I rooted in the vast
repository of my handbag,

I kept it in my mouth,
a sweet-like bulge in the left cheek.
Of those I chose to tell, only two
doubting Thomases wanted proof.

I showed them the eye,
its lustre rinsed away
by the action of my mouth;
grey, a going-off gooseberry.

Arbiter

I hardly knew you then,
couldn't have foreseen
the fork in the road approaching.
I try to think you incidental
to a time and place, the chance
that took us walking late
an Autumn evening onto
a winding drive,
an untended fire burning.

Only the magnetic power
of the hurrying flames against
a background of dark gathering
and us part of a fiery spectacle,
made me incline my head
on your left shoulder, ignore
time, the "No Trespassers" sign,
in the warmth of our enfolding.

What else was being consumed
with wood and leaves,
the hiss of sap protesting
at the heat or unyielding,
ejected in a shower of sparks,
smouldered its shape
to ash at our feet?

"Plane Tree That Ate A Seat"

(Newspaper Heading)

Slowly, imperceptibly, over years
wooden lips swelled and opened mid-trunk
advanced over, under the seats back
wood to tree in backwards evolution

Did those who sat there to rest or think
feel even the faintest spinechafing nibble
sense how time alone saved them.

Raspberry Sauce

I ate the last of summer,
raspberry sauce spooned
from a jar, autumn
rain spattering the window

remembering a seaside outing
scuttled in traffic,
tempers sharp as the glint
of sun on windscreens;

turning off at a sign
"Summer fruits, pick
your own", losing
track of time, moving

along bleached grass
among staked raspberry cane.
That evening a mound
of red berries, next day

sprouting a grey mist.
I picked them over
salvaging the best but
the taste came through.

Spartan Mother

Breeder for the state
she waits
while medics wash
her newborn son in wine;

imperfect or weak
his fate
a laconic nod
towards the abyss.

Hope is a slow judgment,
the cold hillside test.
Forbidden to answer
her bleating lamb,

if he lives out the night,
foolish to hold him close
to be wrenched from her
at seven, to soldier and steal;

if caught,
to be that boy who let
the fox cub hidden in his coat,
eat his innards out.

Indian Woman

(Jimmy Durham Exhibition)

An Indian woman's head
on a catalogue
I pinned to the wall.

Half the face
a totem pole design,
straggly hair, raven-blue.

A bone amulet round a neck
elongated like a donkey's
straining uphill.

Her clear left eye
commands my attention,
pierces me with its message

"Look at me
signed by my race
I do what has to be done"